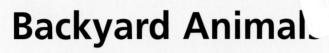

Backyard Animals

Owls

Nick Winnick

MEDIA ENHANCED BOOKS
AV2 BY WEIGL
ADDED VALUE · AUDIO VISUAL

www.av2books.com

BOOK CODE

A823444

AV² by Weigl brings you media enhanced books that support active learning.

AV² provides enriched content that supplements and complements this book. Weigl's AV² books strive to create inspired learning and engage young minds for a total learning experience.

Go to **www.av2books.com**, and enter this book's unique code. You will have access to video, audio, web links, quizzes, a slide show, and activities.

Audio
Listen to sections of the book read aloud.

Video
Watch informative video clips.

Web Link
Find research sites and play interactive games.

Try This!
Complete activities and hands-on experiments.

Due to the dynamic nature of the Internet, some of the URLs and activities provided as part of AV² by Weigl may have changed or ceased to exist. AV² by Weigl accepts no responsibility for any such changes. All media enhanced books are regularly monitored to update addresses and sites in a timely manner. Contact AV² by Weigl at 1-866-649-3445 or av2books@weigl.com with any questions, comments, or feedback.

Published by AV² by Weigl
350 5th Avenue, 59th floor
New York, NY 10118
Website: www.av2books.com   www.weigl.com

Library of Congress Cataloging-in-Publication Data

Winnick, Nick.
 Owls / Nick Winnick.
    p. cm. -- (Backyard animals)
 Includes index.
 ISBN 978-1-60596-952-7 (hardcover : alk. paper) -- ISBN 978-1-60596-953-4 (softcover : alk. paper) --
 ISBN 978-1-60596-954-1 (e-book)
 1. Owls--Juvenile literature. I. Title.
 QL696.S8W56 2010
 598.9'7--dc22

                                2009050307

Printed in the United States of America in North Mankato, Minnesota
1 2 3 4 5 6 7 8 9 0 14 13 12 11 10

042010

WEP264000

Editor Heather C. Hudak   **Design** Terry Paulhus

Every reasonable effort has been made to trace ownership and to obtain permission to reprint copyright material. The publishers would be pleased to have any errors or omissions brought to their attention so that they may be corrected in subsequent printings.

Photo Credits
Weigl acknowledges Getty Images as its primary photo supplier for this title.

Contents

Meet the Owl

Owls are a kind of bird known as a raptor. Raptors hunt small animals and other birds for food. Owls are a large group of birds with many different kinds of **prey**.

Most owls are **nocturnal**. This means they are most active at night and sleep during the day. Owls have special body features that make them better suited to hunting at night. For example, they are silent fliers, so prey cannot hear them. Owls have keen eyesight to help them see small animals in almost complete darkness. An owl's feathers often match the coloring of their surroundings so they cannot be seen easily.

Fascinating Facts

Great horned owls have one of the most well-known hoots. Their "whoo-hoo-ho-o-o" can be heard in natural areas across the United States.

During an Arctic summer, there is almost constant daylight. For this reason, some owls are active during the day as well as at night.

All about Owls

Modern birds belong to one of four groups. Owls, along with doves, hawks, eagles, and most other birds, are part of the group called *neoaves*. This name means "new birds."

There are about 200 different **species** of owls living today. They come in many shapes and sizes. The largest owls are the eagle owls. They can have **wingspans** of 6.6 feet (2 meters). The elf owl is the smallest type of owl. It weighs about 1 ounce (28 grams) and is only 5 inches (13 centimeters) long.

About 19 owl species live in North America.

Owl Wingspans

Common Barn Owl

- Wingspan can be up to 43 inches (109 cm)

Great Horned Owl

- Wingspan is between 36 and 60 inches (91 and 152 cm)

Snowy Owl

- Wingspan is between 54 and 65 inches (137 and 165 cm)

Spotted Owl

- Wingspan can be up to 43 inches (109 cm)

Burrowing Owl

- Wingspan is between 20 and 24 inches (51 and 61 cm).

Eastern Screech Owl

- Wingspan can be up to 22 inches (56 cm)

Owl History

Modern birds developed from a group of dinosaurs called theropods. Some well-known theropods are velociraptors and tyrannosaurus rex.

Theropods first appeared about 230 million years ago. Some small theropods grew feathers to keep them warm. These feathered dinosaurs began to glide, much like flying squirrels do today. Over time, they grew muscles and long feathers to help them fly. This group of theropods survived when all other dinosaurs became **extinct** about 65 million years ago. Over time, they developed into the birds that live today.

Fascinating Facts

A group of owls is called a parliament. This word is also used to describe a group of government officials. Owls were thought to be wise by some cultures.

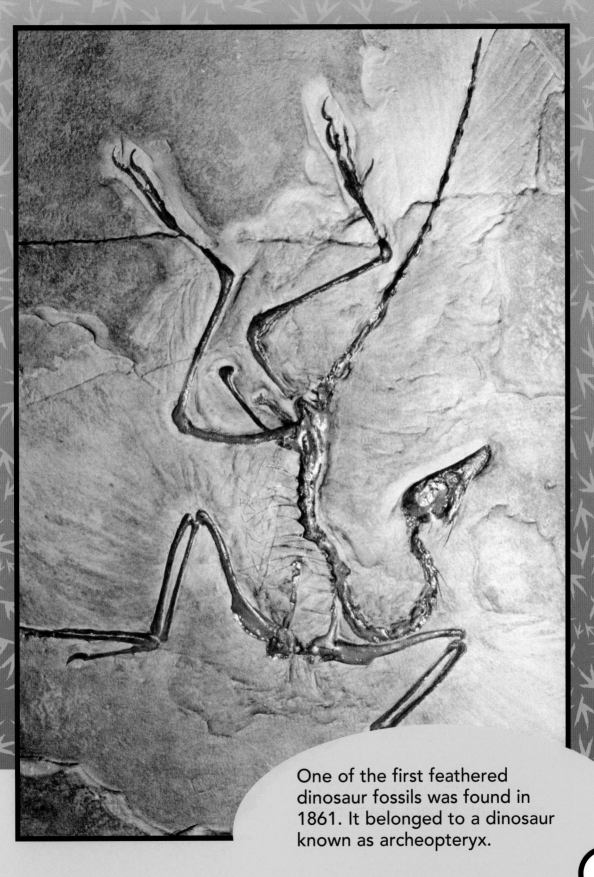

One of the first feathered dinosaur fossils was found in 1861. It belonged to a dinosaur known as archeopteryx.

Owl Shelter

Owls can be found in nearly every country on Earth. They most often live in places that are less than 6,562 feet (2,000 m) above **sea level**. In **tropical** areas, they may live as high as 9,843 feet (3,000 m) above sea level.

Owls have a wide range of **habitats**, from towering forests to hollows in the ground. For example, barn owls hunt in open fields, grasslands, and sparse woodlands. Snowy owls can be found in boreal forests and Arctic **tundras**. Great horned owls live far from human settlements. They make their homes in dense woodlands and along cliffs and canyons. Burrowing owls live on prairies and open plains. They nest in burrows that have been made by badgers, ground squirrels, and other digging animals.

Owls can be found on every continent, except Antarctica.

Owls find different places to sleep, depending on the species and their surroundings. Common places are hollow trees, burrows, and rafters in farm buildings.

Owl Features

Owls have special **adaptations** that help them hunt well at night. For example, owls have very large eyes. This lets them take in as much light as possible to improve their vision at night. Owls' eyes face forward to help them judge distance.

WINGS
Many owls have broad wings that let them glide easily.

FEATHERS
Owl feathers have tiny bristles on the front edges. This muffles the sound they make while flying, letting them move silently.

EYES
Owls are farsighted. They have difficulty seeing past a few inches (5 to 8 cm) in front of their faces. They can see well at night and in daylight.

EARS
An owl's ears point forward. The ears have large openings that are surrounded by feathers. This helps make them more sensitive to sounds. Owls use their hearing to help them catch prey.

NECK
Owls cannot move their eyes in their sockets. They must turn their head to change their view. Owls can turn their head 135 degrees to either side. This lets them look almost directly behind their body. Owls can turn their head in nearly every direction to get a good look at their surroundings.

What Do Owls Eat?

All owls are **predators**. They hunt other animals for food. Owls have a sharp, hook-shaped beak that curves downward. They also have sharp, curved **talons** at the end of each of their four toes. Both the beak and talons are used to catch and tear prey. Many owls eat mice, grasshoppers, and other small creatures.

One of the most impressive hunters is the great horned owl. These owls live throughout North and South America. Great horned owls prey mainly on rabbits, grouse, and ducks. They have been known to hunt geese, skunks, and even porcupines.

Some strong owls tear up large prey before eating it. However, many owls swallow their food whole. Soft parts of the prey are **digested**. Bones, teeth, fur, or feathers are coughed up in bunches known as pellets.

Owls have specially shaped eyes that let in as much light as possible. This lets them hunt well at night.

Scientists study pellets to learn the foods different types of owls eat.

Owl Life Cycle

Owls have many ways of attracting mates and raising their young. Most owls attract mates with their calls and their feathers. In some species, males will offer females a gift of food. A male and female owl will remain together for life.

Eggs

Some owls, such as the great horned owl, may only lay one egg at a time. Other species may lay as many as 12. Most lay three or four. A mated pair of owls will stay together to look after the eggs. Often, the male will hunt, while the female keeps the eggs warm. In some species, these roles are shared.

Owlets

After about two weeks to two months of nesting, the eggs will hatch. A newly hatched owl is called an owlet. One parent will guard the nesting spot, while the other hunts for food. Most owlets are able to fly about a month after hatching. By two months, owlets leave the nesting spot to begin hunting on their own. At as early as four months, owlets are strong fliers and powerful hunters.

Once a pair of owls have mated, they look for a safe place to lay their eggs. Owls do not build nests. They lay their eggs in the nests of other birds, in hollow trees, or on the ground.

Adult

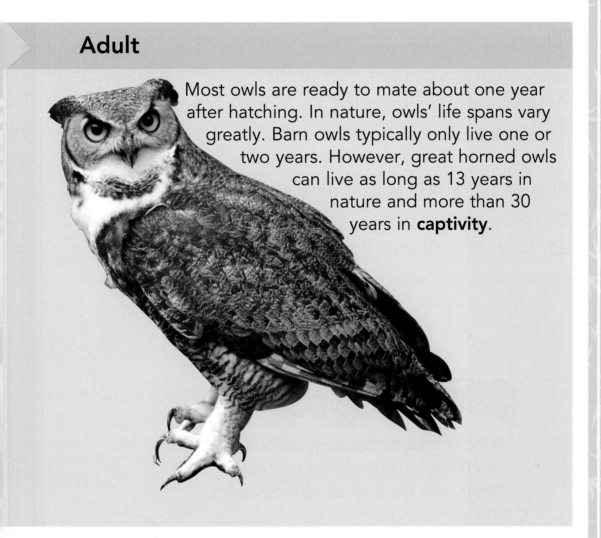

Most owls are ready to mate about one year after hatching. In nature, owls' life spans vary greatly. Barn owls typically only live one or two years. However, great horned owls can live as long as 13 years in nature and more than 30 years in **captivity**.

Encountering Owls

Owls can be dangerous birds. Though they are not known for harming humans, it is best to keep a safe distance from them. In nature, a pair of binoculars lets people get a good look at these beautiful birds without disturbing them.

Shaking trees, shining lights, and making owl calls are common ways to upset these animals. Such upsets can cause changes to their way of life. They may not be able to hunt and feed their babies as they normally would. This can be harmful to the owl.

Disturbing a sleeping or nesting owl could frighten the bird. Great horned owls, for example, can be very aggressive when guarding their eggs. They may try to defend themselves.

Fascinating Facts

Like sharks, great gray owls have a third eyelid. This eyelid protects their eyes from small objects when they attack prey.

Burrowing owls can make the sound of a rattlesnake's rattle to frighten predators.

Myths and Legends

The owl is an important bird in many cultures around the world. People in almost every country have stories about the owl. An owl might be a symbol of good or bad luck, death, or wisdom.

In ancient Greece, the goddess of wisdom, Athena, was often shown with an owl. To this day, owls are a symbol of wisdom to many people.

At one time, people in India would count the hoots of owls to gain clues about the future. One hoot was a symbol of death. Two hoots was a sign of good luck. Three hoots meant there soon would be a wedding in the family.

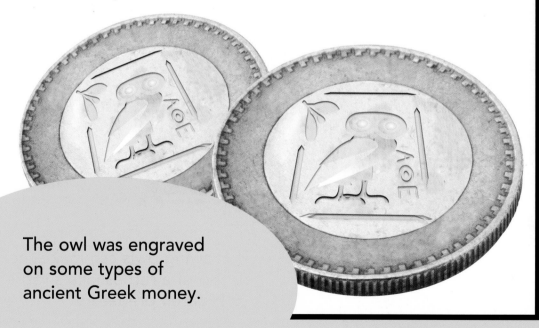

The owl was engraved on some types of ancient Greek money.

Harry and Hedwig

Some cultures believe that owls have mystical powers. Owls were often involved in stories of sorcery and magic. Many stories today include owls that have magical powers. For example, owls are an important part of the Harry Potter series of books and movies.

In Harry Potter's magical world, owls are messengers for witches and wizards. They are prized for their wisdom and skill at finding people. Harry Potter has a snowy owl named Hedwig.

Hedwig is a female owl in the story, but her character is played by male owls in the films. Male snowy owls are nearly pure white, like the one in the movie. Females have dark bands across the chest and wings. Using a male snowy owl to play Hedwig makes it easier for the actors to carry the bird. This is because most male owls weigh slightly less than females.

Frequently Asked Questions

Can owls be helpful to people?

Answer: Yes. Since an owl's main diet is made up of rodents, many farmers raise barn owls. They are used to control rats, mice, and shrews that eat crops.

Do owls have any enemies?

Answer: Most owls have very few enemies. The types of predators depend on the owl species. Smaller owls, such as the burrowing owl, may be hunted by cats or even other birds. Larger owls, such as the great horned owl and snowy owl, have no natural predators. People are a threat to all types of owls. They destroy owls' habitats to put up buildings or to farm the land.

Do all owls hoot?

Answer: No. Depending on the species, owls can make many different sounds. Hoots are the best-known sound owls make. However, screeches, cries, and shrieks also are common sounds made by owls.

Words to Know

adaptations: changes in animals that help them survive in their environment

captivity: not living in a natural habitat

digested: broken down by the body and used for nourishment

extinct: an entire species of animals with no living members

habitats: natural living places

nocturnal: mainly active at night

predators: animals that hunt other animals for food

prey: animals that are hunted by other animals for food

sea level: the surface of the sea

species: a group of animals with the same characteristics; members of a species can usually only breed with other members of that species

talons: sharp claws found on certain birds

tropical: a warm area near the equator

tundras: arctic plains with small plants and frozen ground

wingspans: the width of a bird's wings, from tip to tip, when they are spread out

Index

Log on to www.av2books.com

AV² by Weigl brings you media enhanced books that support active learning. Go to **www.av2books.com**, and enter the special code inside the front cover of this book. You will gain access to enriched and enhanced content that supplements and complements this book. Content includes video, audio, web links, quizzes, a slide show, and activities.

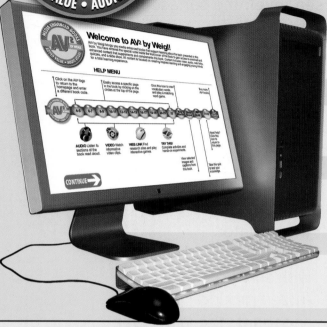

Audio
Listen to sections of the book read aloud.

Video
Watch informative video clips.

Web Link
Find research sites and play interactive games.

Try This!
Complete activities and hands-on experiments.

WHAT'S ONLINE?

Try This! Complete activities and hands-on experiments.	**Web Link** Find research sites and play interactive games.	**Video** Watch informative video clips.	**EXTRA FEATURES**
Pages 6-7 Identify types of owls.	**Pages 6-7** Find out more about owl features.	**Pages 4-5** Watch a video about how to identify owls.	 **Audio** Hear introductory audio at the top of every page
Pages 12-13 List five important features of owls.	**Pages 8-9** Learn about theropods.	**Pages 10-11** See a burrowing owl in its natural habitat.	**Key Words** Study vocabulary, and play a matching word game.
Pages 16-17 Compare the similarities and differences between an owlet and an adult owl.	**Pages 10-11** Play an interactive owl game.	**Pages 14-15** Watch a video about a snowy owl hunting.	**Slide Show** View images and captions, and try a writing activity.
Page 22 Test your owl knowledge.	**Pages 18-19** Find out fascinating facts about owls.		**AV² Quiz** Take this quiz to test your knowledge
	Pages 20-21 Read more stories about owls.		